Goldie,
A beautiful young Lady!
Love,
Lynnette

God Bless You Goldie
Judy Plumley

Heaven
How To Live Til We Get There

By Lynnette Maynor • Illustrated by Judy Plumley

Graphic Design & Book Formatting by Starry Eyes Media, Oak Hill, WV
www.StarryEyesMedia.com

All rights reserved solely by the author. The author guarantees all contents are original and do not infringe upon the legal rights of any other person or work. No part of this book may be reproduced in any form without the permission of the author.

Scripture quotations taken from the King James Version (KJV), New King James Version (NKJV), New International Version (NIV) and International Children's Bible (ICB).
New Living Translation (NLT) – public domain.

Copyright © 2017 Lynnette Maynor

...For Him...

There is a kingdom that is holy
and royal beyond compare.
A place of light and purity;
no sin can enter there.

A place of love, peace and joy
where everyone is free;
from anything that ever hurt them
for all eternity.

It's Ruler is The Almighty.
He is God The King.
He rules with love and kindness,
Forever His praises ring.

This is the place called heaven;
the beautiful city above,
made of gold and sparkling jewels
because of God's great love.

Jesus said..."In My Father's house are many mansions";
... "I go to prepare a place for you". - John 14:2

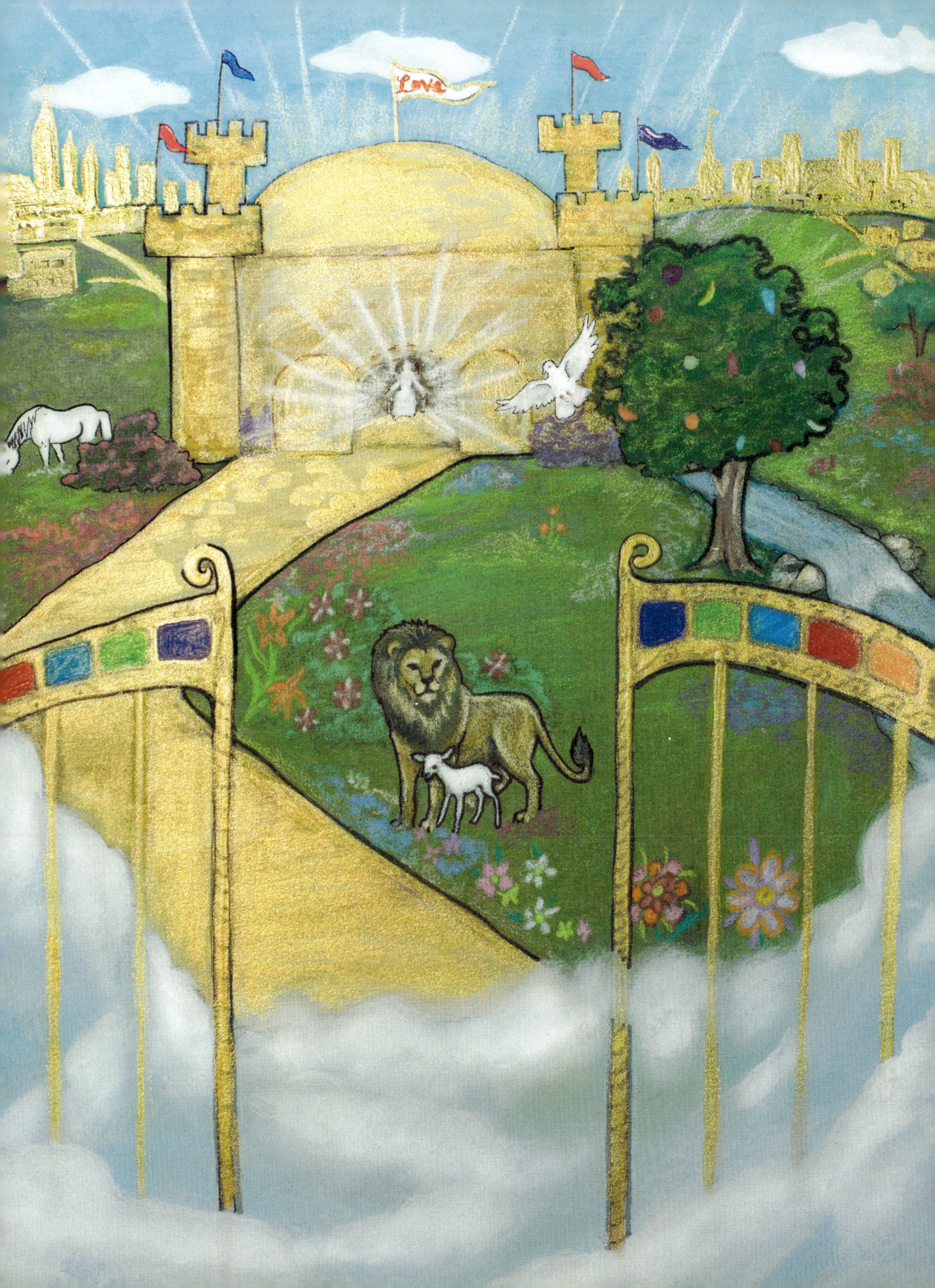
Love

Those who live in this city
are dressed in purest white.
They're made clean by the blood of Jesus,
Who is now in their present sight.

To live in this amazing heaven
comes from a decision we make on earth.
We must accept Jesus as our Savior.
We're given life through this new birth.

We must believe Jesus died on the cross
and rose up from the grave.
When we say "yes" and receive Him,
all our sins are removed and we're saved.

Then God becomes our Father
when we accept Jesus His Perfect Son.
His Holy Spirit comes to live in us
and in Christ we are made one.

"...as many as received Him, to them He gave the right to become children of God, to those who believe in His name." - John 1:12

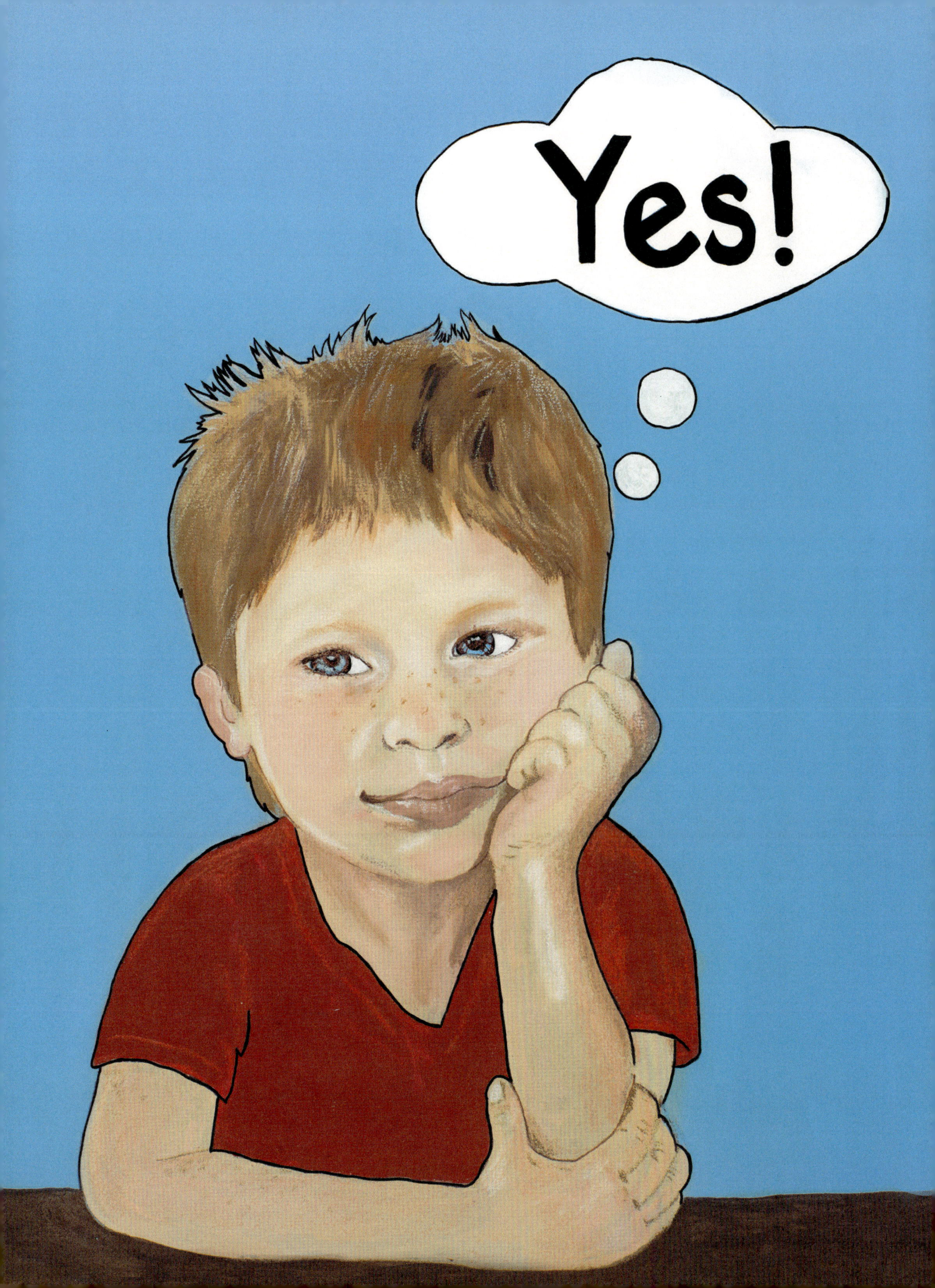
Yes!

*O*nce you've accepted Jesus
and He lives inside your heart;
You'll want to know about Him
right from the very start.

*B*ecause knowing more about Him
helps you live a life that's true;
loving Him, yourself and others,
just to name a few.

*L*ove is the greatest,
this we surely know.
The meaning of love is God.
The Bible tells us so.

*U*ntil we go to heaven,
as we live upon the earth;
God's gives us everything we need
to live in victory since our new birth.

"...God is love..." - *I John 4:16*
"...Thanks be to God, who always leads us in victory through Christ..." - *II Corinthians 2:14*

Love

God gives us special armor
and covers us in light.
We never have to be afraid
of even the darkest night.

Even though we may not see it,
we wear it just the same;
given to all who accept Jesus;
who gladly bear His name.

This armor protects from an enemy;
one who is very real.
Satan is always trying to hurt us;
to lie to us and steal.

He wants to take God's truths from us,
stealing our peace inside.
But God is our protection;
in Him we live and abide.

So always please remember;
this you can know for sure;
the power of God is greater
and in this we are safe and secure.

"Put on the whole armor of God, that you may be able to stand against the wiles (tricks) of the devil." - Ephesians 6:11

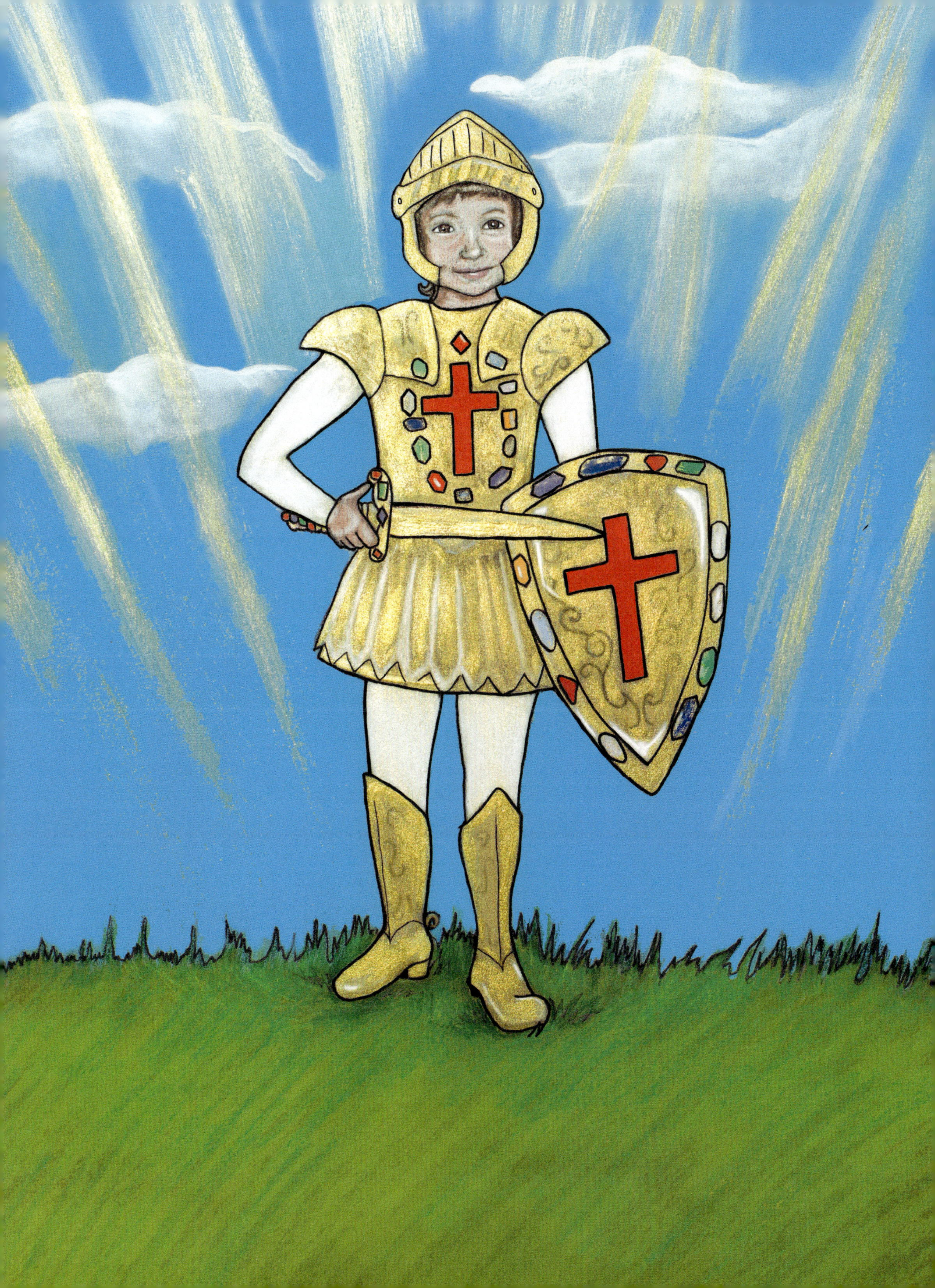

Now that you know of this enemy,
you'll want to be real strong;
like a tree with roots so very deep,
your earthly whole life long.

Because roots which grow so deeply
help a tree stand very tall;
when winds and storms blow all around
it won't topple and fall.

We're kind of like trees, sometimes we feel shaken;
some things we just don't understand;
Then we remember God is holding us
and has us by the hand.

We're reminded God has a plan for us;
one that is very good.
The next few pages will explain to you
how to live life as you should.

"...be strong in the Lord and in the power of His might." - *Ephesians 6:10*
"I know the plans I have for you", declares The Lord, "...plans to give you hope and a future." - *Jeremiah 29:11*

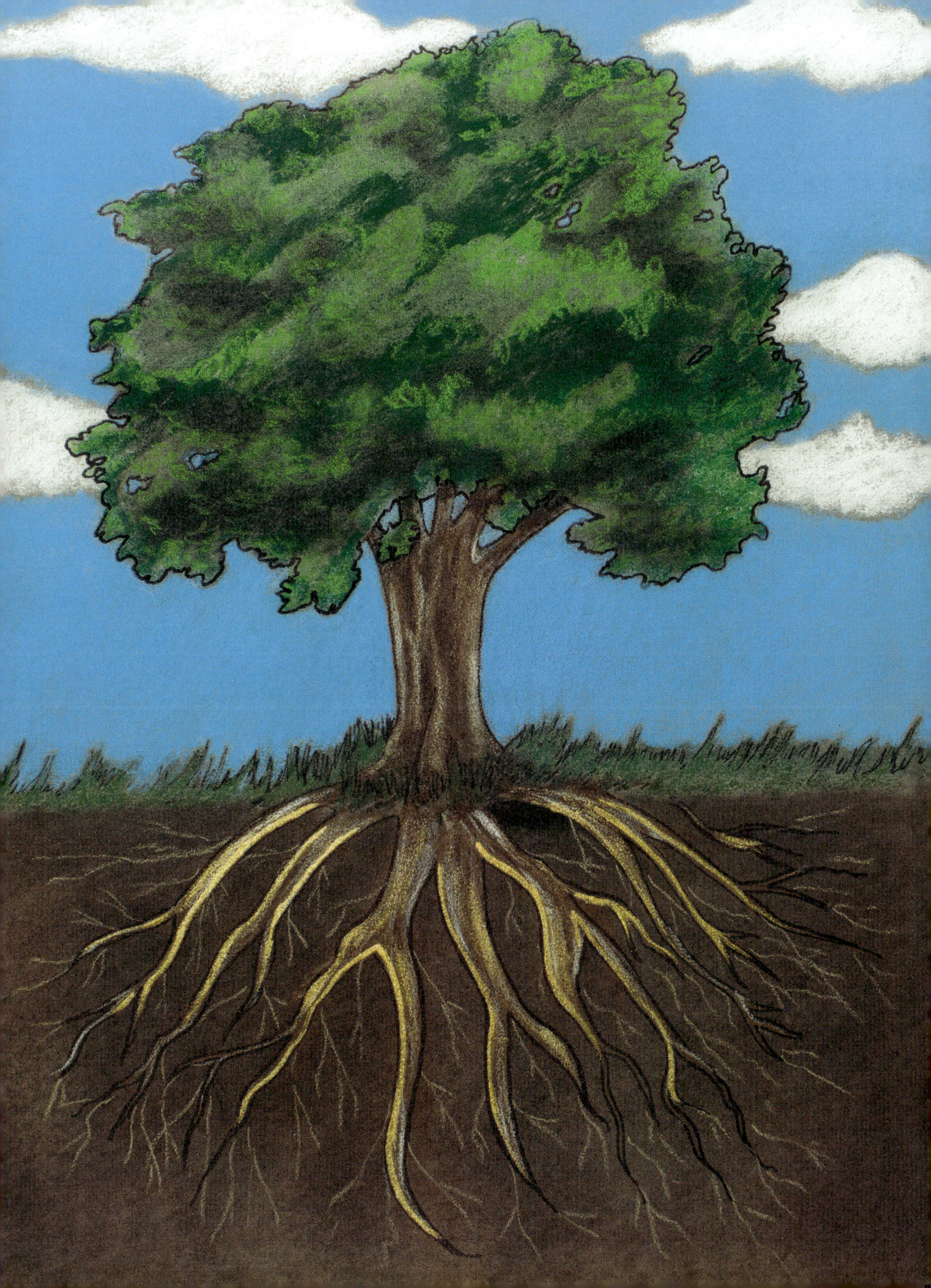

Let us start with the Bible;
it is God's word we know;
His very special love letter to us;
Telling how He loves us so.

It's like our instruction book,
showing us how to live;
a life of love, peace and joy;
a life that is happy and gives.

His word is living and powerful;
such a strong defense;
when Satan tries to lie to us,
some moments can be very tense.

When this begins to happen
and he tries to attack our mind,
we remember the words of the Bible
and our peace we immediately find.

God's Holy Spirit reminds us
that every thing's okay;
that He is always with us
and He'll never go away.

"...the word of God is living and powerful, and sharper than any two-edged sword..." - Hebrews 4:12
"Let this mind be in you which was also in Christ Jesus..." - Philippians 2:5

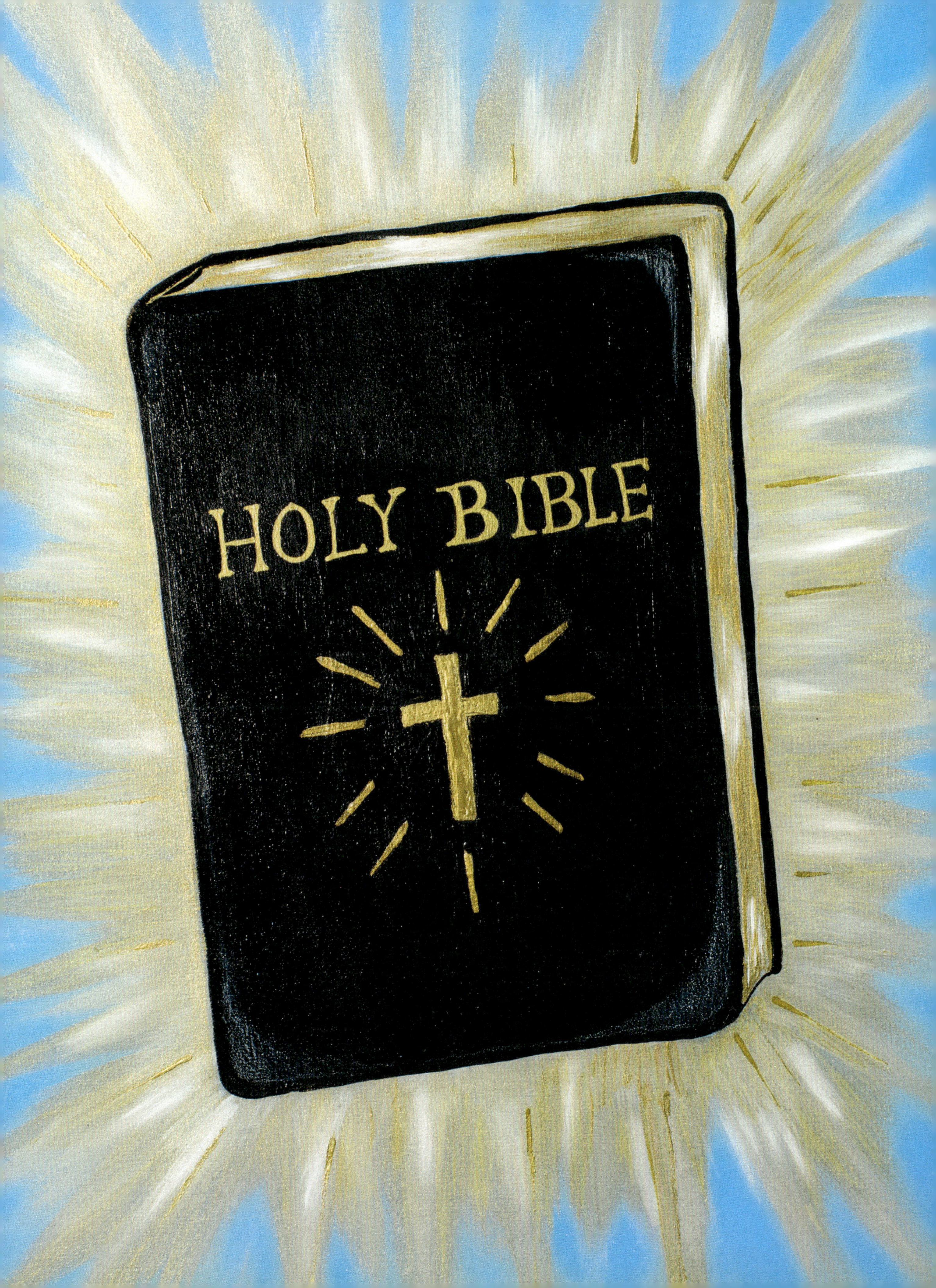
HOLY BIBLE

It's always good to talk to God.
That's what it means to pray.
We speak to Him about everything,
then listen to what He has to say.

Spending time each day with Him
helps us clearly see;
The heart of God and what pleases Him;
then more like Him we'll be.

We talk to Him like a father.
He is our closest friend.
Our dear and loving friendship
is one that will never end.

It always brings us comfort
knowing He is there;
to talk to every moment,
knowing how much He cares.

"...pray continually." - I Thessalonians 5:17

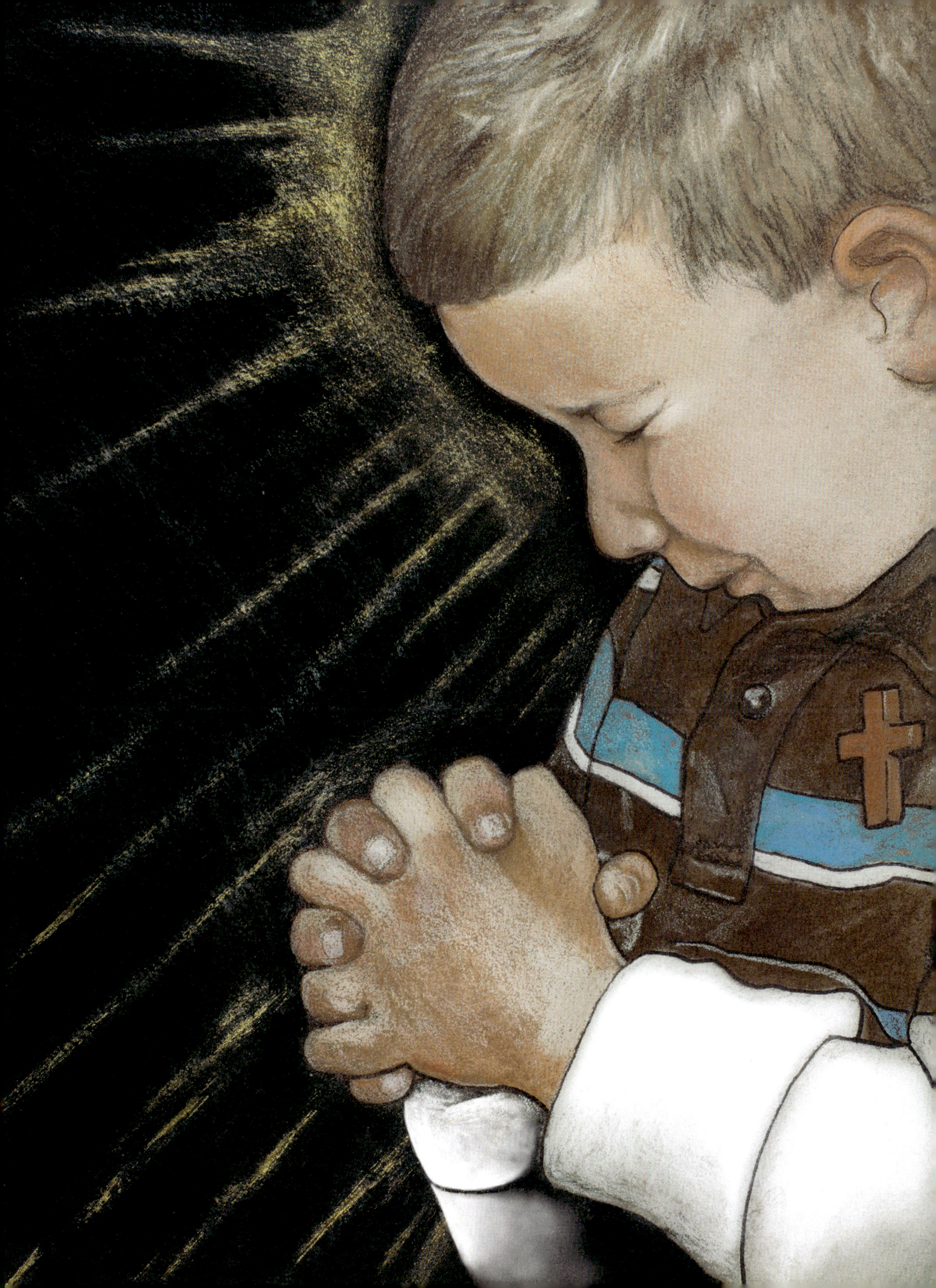

There's a special place to visit;
a place to often go
to learn more about God's Word
and be reminded how He loves us so.
This place is called the church,
a caring place to be;
where we join with others
who love God like you and me.
God told us to be together
a long, long time ago;
because it makes us stronger
and helps our faith to grow.
When we meet together as one,
meaning we're all in one accord.
It gives God great honor
and says that He is Lord.

"Let us think of ways to motivate one another to acts of love and good works. And let us not neglect our meeting together, as some people do, but encourage one another, especially now that the day of His return is drawing near." - Hebrews 10:24-25

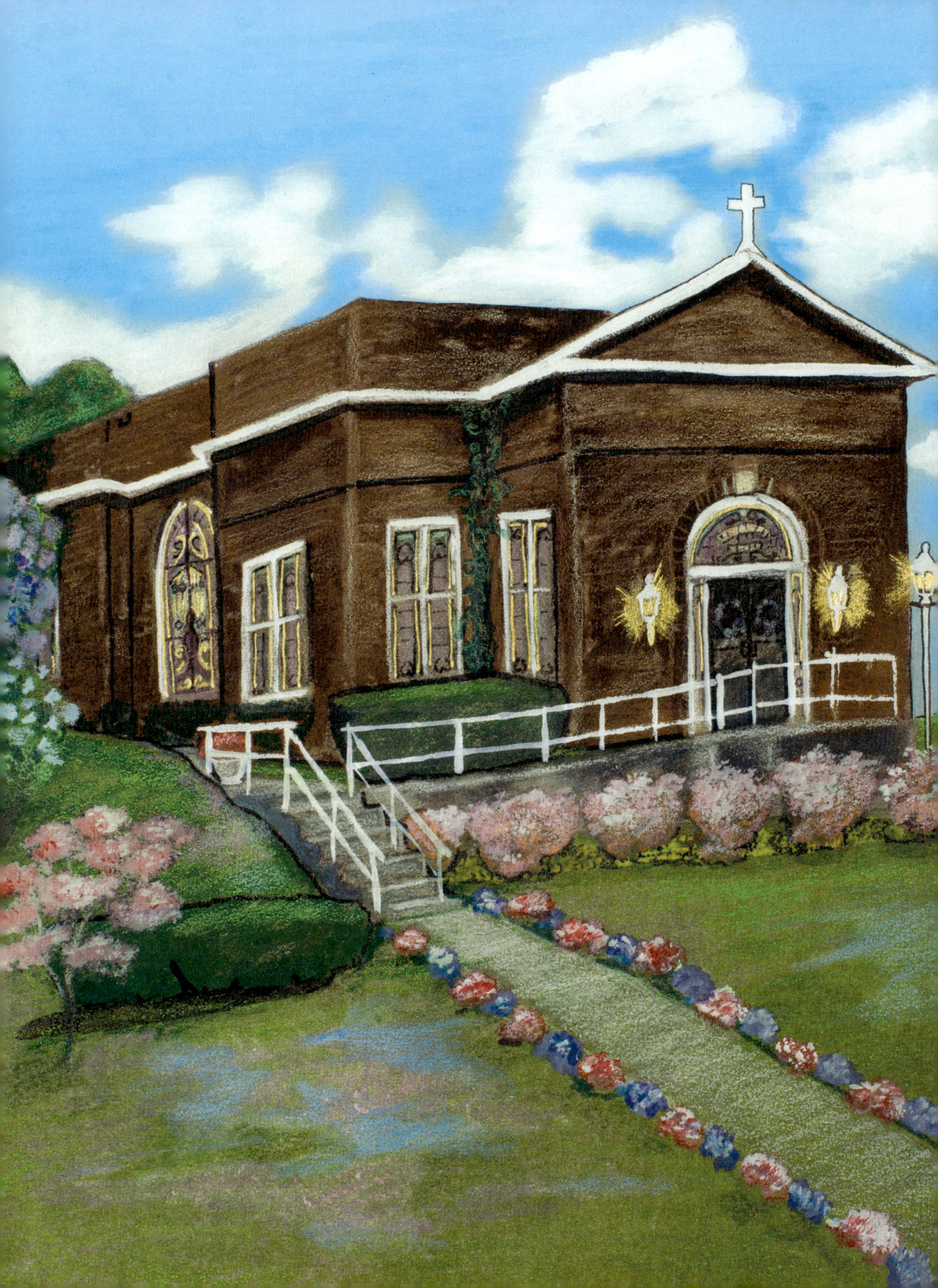

There is something so powerful,
I'm sure you'd like to know.
It is praise and worship;
telling God we love Him so.

God is so amazing and wonderful
and absolutely adored.
That's where praise and worship begins;
knowing He is Lord.

When you give honor to God,
it puts a smile upon His face;
He then moves mightily
and peace takes worry's place.

Your problems begin to melt away
or they won't matter as much.
When you speak of His greatness,
He brings an amazing healing touch.

You can celebrate the greatness of God
in many different ways.
You can sing, clap, lift your hands,
dance or shout His praise.

Sometimes you're very quiet and still;
you're amazed and thinking wow!
A God like Him is so awesome,
you just worship and bow.

"I will bless the Lord at all times; His praise shall continually be in my mouth." - Psalm 34:1
"Oh, worship the Lord in the beauty of holiness!" - Psalm 96:9

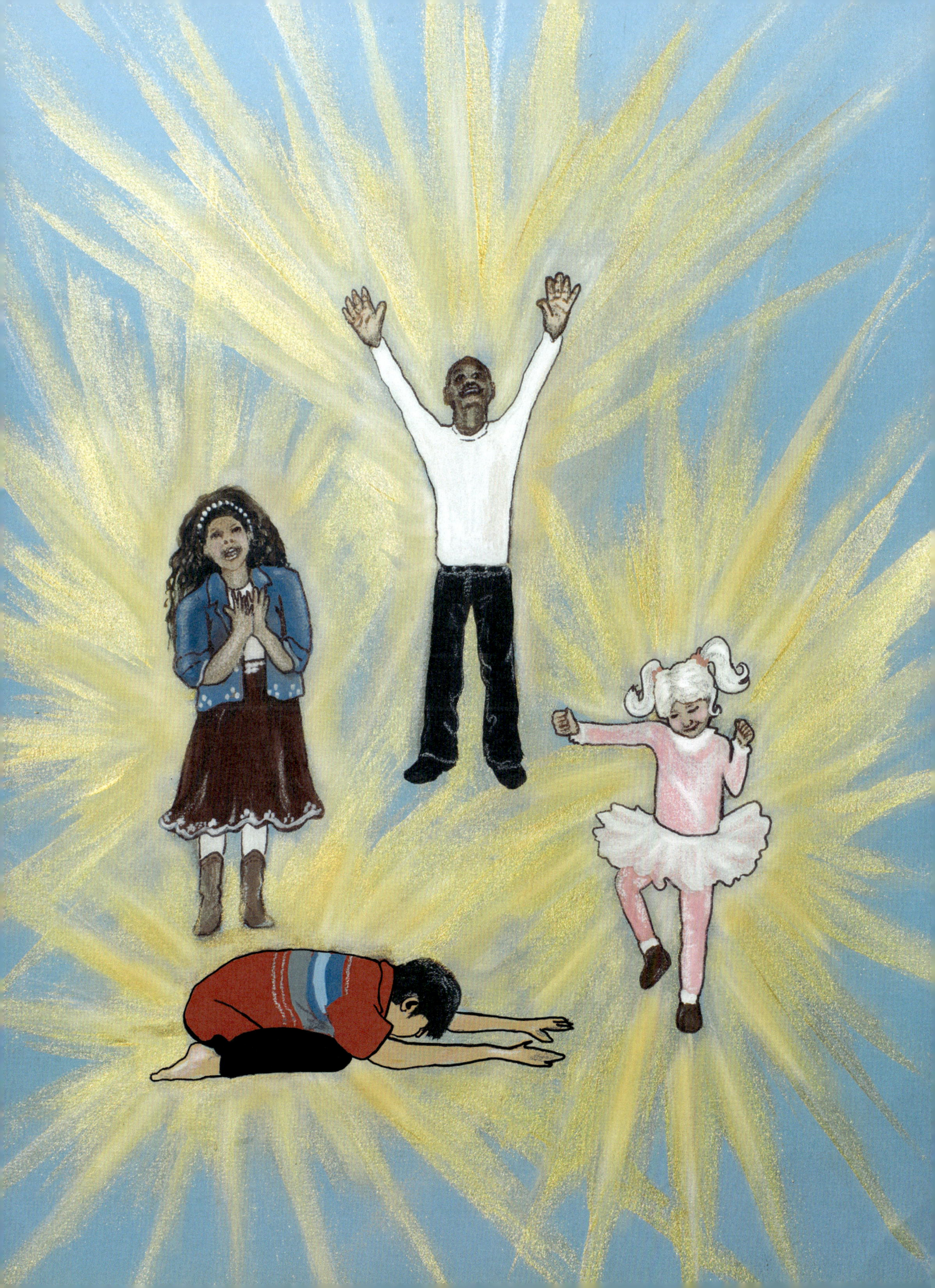

Until we go to heaven
to be with God above;
He wants us to tell everyone
of His amazing love.

He tells us to share His good news;
to speak of Jesus' fame;
so others may accept Him as Savior
and have forgiveness in His name.

Once they come to know Him,
they will realize;
That He lives inside them
and heaven is their prize.

They'll be so very happy
when their sins are washed away;
by the Blood of Jesus
and knowing He's there to stay.

Jesus said, "Go everywhere in the world. Tell the Good News to everyone." - Mark 16:15
"For God so loved the world that He gave His only begotten Son,
that whoever believes in Him should not perish but have everlasting life." - John 3:16

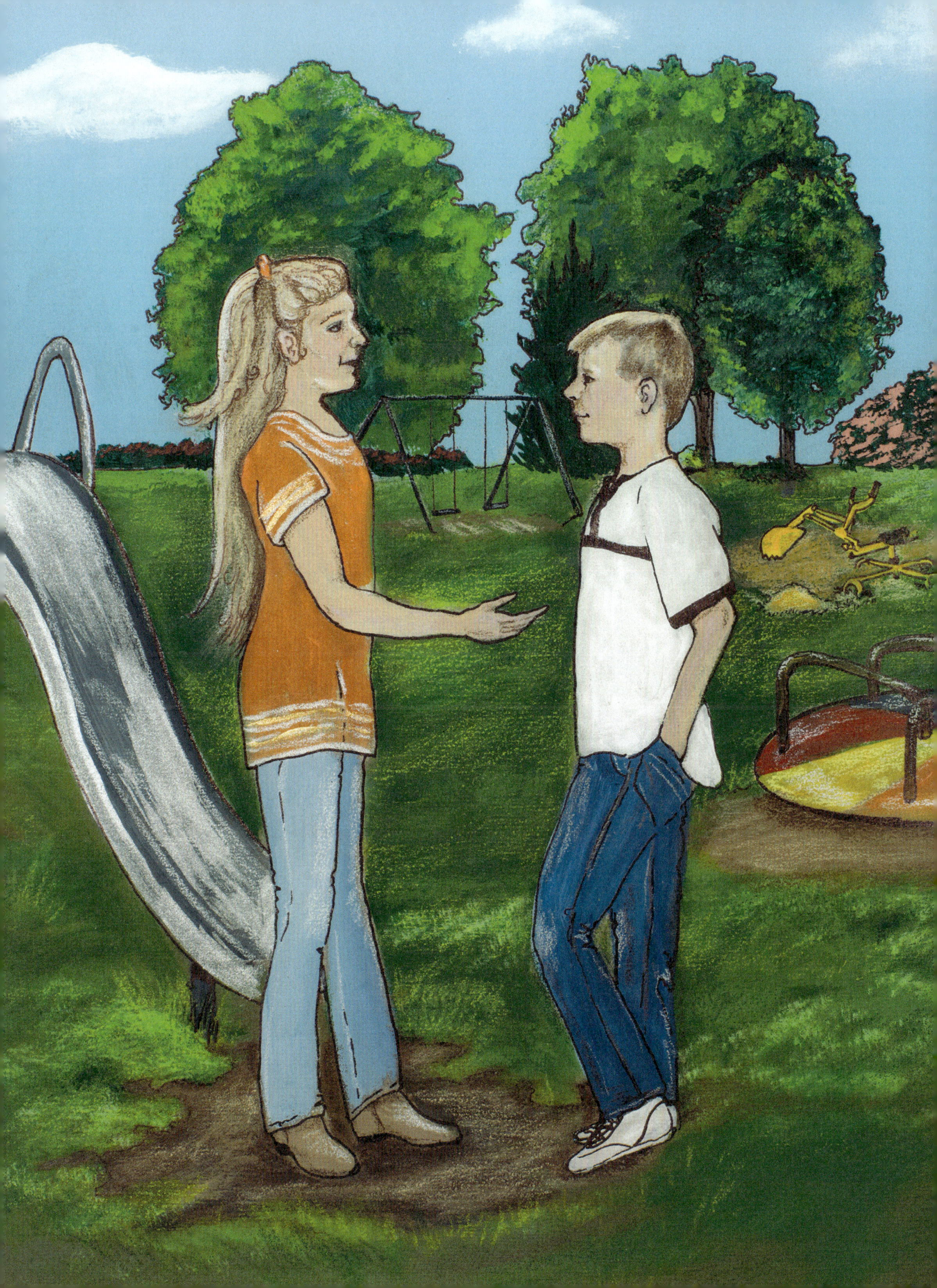

This wonderful heaven we've spoken of
is for you and me.
God wants us to live there
through all eternity.

Now is the time for deciding
if heaven is what you chose;
to be with God forever;
to win and never lose.

Jesus says, "Come to Me;
come to Me and live;
and be with Me forever,
in the beautiful heaven I give.

Because I am the Savior;
I am the only way;
please accept me as your Lord"
Here is what you say:

Jesus said, "I am the way, the truth, and the life: no man cometh unto the Father, but by Me." - John 14:6

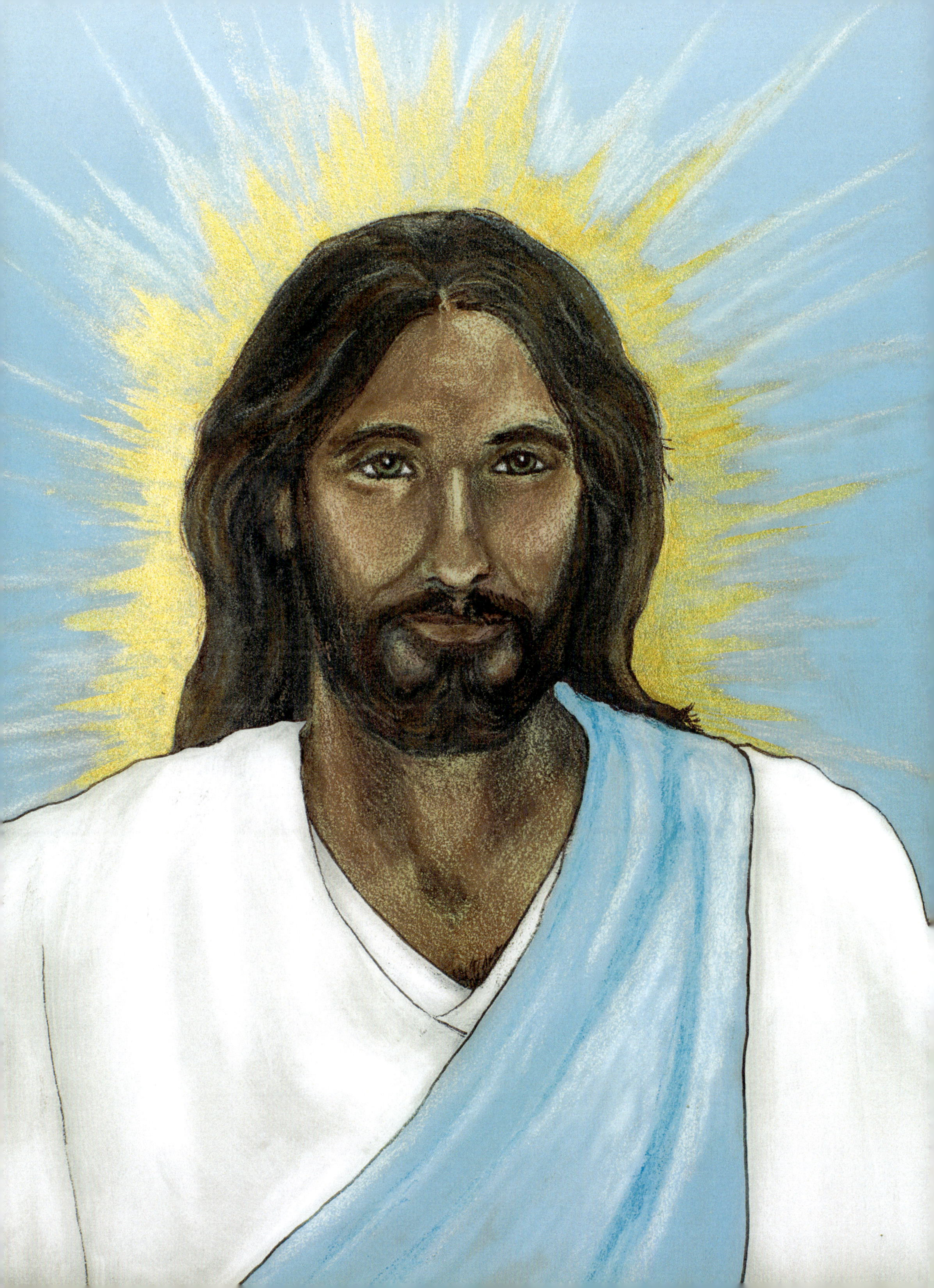

Dear God,

I know I have sinned, done wrong things, and I am sorry. I believe Jesus died on the cross for my sins and came back to life. I open my heart and invite You into my life now. Thank You for forgiving me and washing away all my sins with the blood of Jesus.

Thank you for hearing my prayer and coming into my life. Thank You for loving me! I love You too!

"...Christ may dwell in your hearts through faith..." - Ephesians 3:17

*O*nce you receive Him as Savior;
a Friend He will always be;
guiding, protecting and comforting you
forever through eternity.

*I*t will seem He's right beside you
even though He lives inside;
it's like He takes you by the hand;
in Him you live and abide.

*Y*ou'll smile and be so happy
knowing He is there;
to listen and to love you,
giving you tender care.

*Y*ou are very special to Him.
He made only one of you.
He will show you how to live
and even help you too.

"I will instruct you and teach you in the way you should go; I will guide you with My eye." - Psalm 32:8
"I will never leave you nor forsake you." - Hebrews 13:5

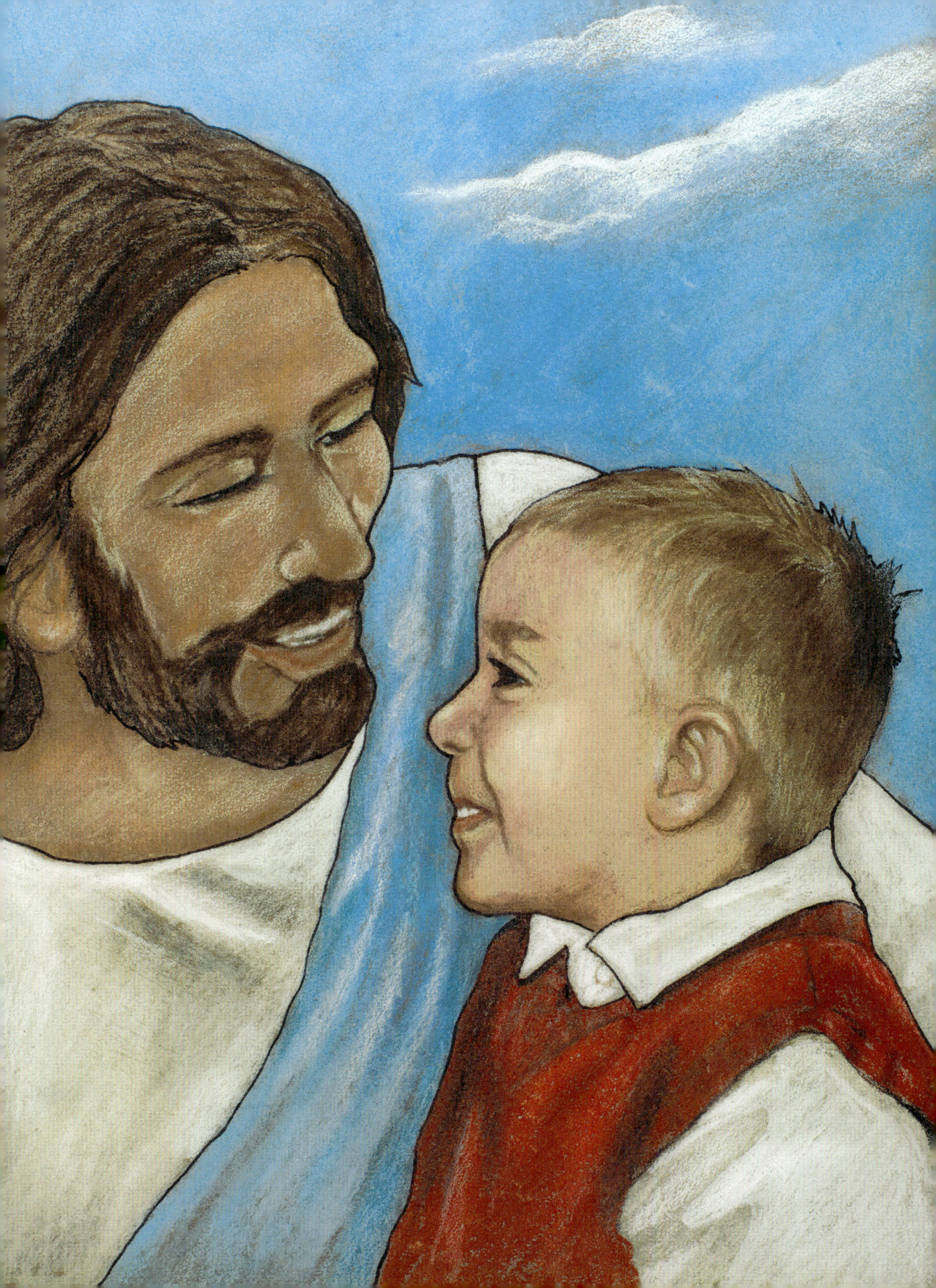

Additional Scripture References

"For all have sinned, and come short of the glory of God."

- Romans 3:2

"Christ died for our sins...He was buried...He rose again the third day according to the scriptures."

- I Corinthians 15:3-4

"You are not redeemed with corruptible things...but with the precious blood of Christ."

- I Peter 1:18-19

"If we confess our sins, He is faithful and just to forgive us our sins, and to cleanse us from all unrighteousness."

- I John 1:9

"...if thou shalt confess with thy mouth the Lord Jesus, and shalt believe in thine heart that God hath raised Him from the dead, thou shalt be saved. For with the heart man believeth unto righteousness; and with the mouth confession is made unto salvation."

- Romans 10:9-10

"For by grace are ye saved through faith; and that not of yourselves: it is the gift of God."

- Ephesians 2:8

Made in the USA
Lexington, KY
20 August 2017